# How Memories Insist

# How Memories Insist

POEMS

MIRNA HIRSCHL

Dancing Leaves Press
2022

Copyright © 2022
Mirna Hirschl
All Rights Reserved.

---

Dancing Leaves Press
ISBN Number 978-1-7342742-1-9

# Credits

The epigraph "Solitude is to the spirit what food is for the body" from Lucius Seneca the Younger, 4th century BCE, accompanying "Listening to Seneca" on page 36, has been excerpted from the public domain.

On page 41, the author Mirna Hirschl has translated from Croatian a fragment of the 1895 poem "Maslina" (Olive Tree) by Vladimir Nazor, excerpted from the public domain.

In "Wanton Words" on page 98, the lines " Something there is that doesn't love a wall" and "To please the yelping dogs" are excerpted from the poem "Mending Wall" by Robert Frost from *North of Boston* (New York: Henry Holt and Company, 1919) in the public domain.

++++

The poem "I Am Old But Do Not Feel So" on page 136 was published in *Celebrate Creativity: Cupertino Community Anthology*, Legentibus Publishing Company, 2020. I am grateful to Keacey McCormick, Cupertino Poet Laureate, 2018-2020, for including it.

For my beloved family
my husband Simon
our children and grandchildren
— my life-song

# Foreword

This collection of poems is a memoir of a remarkable life, a necklace made from "pearl-words" pursued through a "lavish spread of a field." The poet tells us: "I am overdue/to speak with the voice of memories."

She started writing poetry late in life and did so in English, her second language. It is fortunate we can now read her story presented to us as poetry.

The cover photograph is a scarred mimosa tree from her neighborhood. It is also the subject of a poem "The Mimosa on Avon Street" found in the book in which she transforms this image into a tree of knowledge, a knowledge hard-earned from a chain of "unexplained memories," a knowledge earned from family having been carted away, earned in the disappearance of relatives from "guilt-flushed fields of poppies," earned from a single treasured button that "survived in a round pink-lidded case ... meant to hold a jewel."

Under the gaze of the Mimosa tree with its gaping knots that stare through their losses, the poet reminds us that tragedy of war and genocide can ebb into love. She tells us of her hope the tree will bloom again, and she shows us how she celebrated the coming of many springs with the family she built for herself in her new home in the United States.

We get to know about her loves, the sweet anchor of her husband, their children and grandchildren. She takes us on her travels, to the old neighborhoods peopled with figures from the past, on her walks around her current neighborhood and the world she now inhabits.

Past, present, and future are alive in her. And that is the thing—this is a woman on fire with poetry, alive with adoration for words that blossom out of these pages.

She is someone who didn't give in to lethargy despite the seeds of disaster she knows about first-hand, that seems to be taking root in her beloved chosen country.

When she looks into herself she sees a girl in "white knee socks." She instructs us on how to be open to and accept age with this wisdom from "Seed Pods Under My Feet":

> look inward, indulge in the fruit
>
> intact in your heart. Open wide
> your wrinkled hands—words
>
> buried deep between the slits
> of arthritic joints, live there
>
> precariously like wild columbine
> ardently embracing steep cliffs—
>
> do not let them slip—support them
> with synonyms and similes ...

She asks her family and us, her readers, to remember her for the way she raised her kids, for the grandmother she is, for the "aroma of the cakes" she bakes, for the kindness she lavishes on her beloveds and strangers, too.

And just our luck, she is right here with us—to cherish and admire. To write as many poems as she can, as only a beacon of light and inspiration would keep doing, word by leaping word.

    —Phyllis Klein, poet, *The Full Moon Herald*,
       Grayson Books, 2020.

# Contents

**Foreword**     vii

**Chapter 1    How They Get Written**

    Pearl-Words     5
    Wild Strawberries in Winter     6
    How to Draw Warmth     7

**Chapter 2    Why They Must Be Heard**

    A Bridge to Memories     11
    Tales of a Walnut Tree     12
    Four Hoofs of a Fawn     14
    For His Parents' Sake     16
    Epitaph     18
    The Niece's Lament     20

**Chapter 3    In the Teeth of Wintry Sun**

    In the Teeth of Wintry Sun     25
    Heirloom     26
    Splendor in the Kitchen     28
    For the Family Lore     30
    End of a Gravelly Road     32
    In Honor of the Cliché:     34
       How Times Have Changed
    Listening to Seneca     36

**Chapter 4    Figs, Hazelnuts, Muscat Grapes**

    Olive Tree (*Maslina*)     41
    Istria of Yore     42
    The Village Malena     44
    A Blue Fan     46
    A War Widow     48
    Sunday Bread     50

## Chapter 5    Love, What Else?

| | |
|---|---|
| Conundrum | 55 |
| A Love Song | 56 |
| Orlando | 58 |
| Crescendo | 60 |
| Joy | 61 |
| Nasturtium Dreams | 62 |
| Portrait of Baka | 63 |

## Chapter 6    The Roots of Things

| | |
|---|---|
| Bitter Herbs | 67 |
| Following a Rainbow | 68 |
| In the Space of Fantasy | 69 |
| A Tale of Trastevere | 70 |
| Immigrant Silver | 72 |
| The Roots of Things | 73 |

## Chapter 7    Letting Go

| | |
|---|---|
| Fugue | 77 |
| Walking in Belmont | 78 |
| Letting Go | 80 |
| The Mimosa on Avon Street | 82 |
| Terrace After the Rain | 84 |
| A Visit to Paly High School | 86 |

## Chapter 8    Ultimate Nightmare

| | |
|---|---|
| Cruel Dawn | 91 |
| Ultimate Nightmare | 92 |
| A Missing Instrument | 94 |
| A Glimmer of Hope | 96 |
| Wanton Words | 98 |

## Chapter 9  Of Different Strengths

| | |
|---|---|
| Dancing on a Spider Web | 101 |
| Web in a Brave New World | 102 |
| Of Different Strengths | 104 |
| Calm After the Storm | 105 |
| At the Edge of Irony | 106 |

## Chapter 10  A Spread of Wings

| | |
|---|---|
| Lofty on the Horizon | 111 |
| The White Knee Socks | 112 |
| Santorini | 114 |
| Icarus | 116 |
| Kapnikarea | 118 |
| Fado | 120 |

## Chapter 11  Bending Boundaries

| | |
|---|---|
| Subliminal | 123 |
| Stay Unresolved and I Will Love You | 124 |
| Bending Boundaries | 126 |
| The Vagaries of Consonants | 127 |
| The Poetry of Decimal Numbers | 130 |

## Chapter 12  Turning a New Leaf

| | |
|---|---|
| With Open Hands | 135 |
| I Am Old But Do Not Feel So | 136 |
| Turning a New Leaf | 138 |
| A Beautiful Confluence | 140 |
| Passage | 142 |
| Seed Pods Under My Feet | 143 |

**Notes** — 147

**Acknowledgements** — 149

# Poems

How memories insist
a phoenix, still trembling
a field without a fence

# Chapter 1

## How They Get Written

*I will search the forest
for wild strawberries in winter*

## PEARL-WORDS

When they spill
they clink—
pearls in a broken necklace—

they bounce and laugh
roll away and
escape

Playful
pearl-words
I'll pursue you through

a lavish spread of a field
and the silk
of a cornhusk

and when I find you
I'll restring you
into an echo of my soul

## WILD STRAWBERRIES IN WINTER

Now that I have found the music
I am losing the notes.
O cruel fate, why do you mock me so?

When I was young I climbed the tree of living,
blind to the branches in my eagerness—
my mind numb, my tongue tied,
I was happy in complacency.

I have found the potion that quenches my
thirst—this clear mountain brook so sweet
these poems coursing through my veins
must not stay mute for the lack of words
that escape me.

O Euterpe,
I will suffer sleepless nights and pass
my days in haze, only, hold my paintbrush
lend me your double flute, help me find
the precious words, speak them coherently
and I will be your willing slave.

I will wait all night to welcome the buds
as they open at dawn. I will comb an orchard
for the blush of the first apple of the season.

Like in a fairy tale, I will search the forest
for wild strawberries in winter
and lay them at your temple, in humility.

In the final and belated recognition
O my siren, giving much delight
do with me what you will.

## HOW TO DRAW WARMTH

Birds are mounting
A special performance in the blossoming plum tree
Some dart over branches dancing a quadrille
Some perch on a particular twig
Quietly showing off their finery

Come to think of it
It is I who deem it a performance
They are just delighted by the scent of spring
Balmy, cozy with a touch of breeze

Cheeks caressed
Warm from sheer pleasure, dazed
I lean on the wooden fence
It also feels warm and friendly—
The whole world is warm and friendly
I want it to stay like this forever
I wish it, I will it
But will it?

I run inside quickly
For some pen and paper and a fine-tipped charcoal
To draw a garland of delicate plum buds
But how to draw the warmth?

A poem might do it!
Back outside, I lean on the warm fence
My face feels caressed
Ah, yes, that will do it

# Chapter 2

## Why They Must Be Heard

*I am overdue to speak
with the voice of memories*

## A BRIDGE TO MEMORIES

Why in such a rush to spill?
I know not of impending ill
nor abrupt ending

The beads in my necklace
feel firm and tight—
why then this flight

into days, almost forgotten
that are perhaps
best left undisturbed

but then
who would know of them
who honor them?

A bridge is not gone
when the footsteps die
My satisfied life

will no longer do:
I am overdue
to speak with the voice

of memories
and in this
I simply have no choice

## TALES OF A WALNUT TREE
*To Paula, my first friend*

1
Around the walnut tree the grass was plush
a sprawling pillow of soft summer shade;
there pretty Nezzie, the lisp of her nickname
a souvenir of happier days, sat alone and
brooded, and regretted.

Today her husband sought her again and said:
*Look Nezzie, I brought you a basket of fresh strawberries*
She answered: *No, thank you* and chilled his soul.
He knew she wanted to ask: *where were you last night*
but the words would not pass her embittered lips.
He left the basket on the grass; she left it to the birds.

2
Under the same walnut tree, their naughty
son offered a plum brandy to a willing goat
that lapped it up and butted its ebony horns
into a living tree until they broke and oozed
a trail of blood down the carved up trunk.
They whipped the boy, and all three of them
the boy, the goat, and the trunk, remained scarred.

3
Years later I, the granddaughter, fingered the
misshapen grooves of wounded walnut bark
waiting for a friend who never came. *It was
the last night's air-raid that killed the girl next door*
the neighbors said and pointed toward a hole
in the ground, huge, gaping and confirming
malevolent, unforgettable. The tree split in half;
the flying earth bared the roots and shaped them
into spikes of a broken wheel arrested in midair.

4
Seventy years ago we shelled walnuts together;
their unripe, bitter skin stained ours with iodine
that turned rusty brown. That's all I can remember—
no face, only stained fingers and a name.
Only Paula.

## FOUR HOOFS OF A FAWN
*Sarajevo, Summer 1942*

Allusions wove a spooky veil
under dinner conversation.
They haunted me all the way home.

Swinging feather-light
in my parents' honey-warm hands
in four years of organdy blouses
and a large bow on top of a curly bob
I heard Sounds slither through darkness.

Silvery fish somersaulted in my ears—
volumes of vowels slid down the tunnels
riotously fluting, invisible owls
hooting to the beat of premonition.

I cried, gripped by fear. How I cried!

They let me down gently:
*We cannot hear anything.*
*Must be your imagination.*
Then they quickened their steps
to make it home before curfew.

In that unacknowledged night
I was not consoled.
Four hoofs of a fawn
leapt over the fence
of four years of innocence.

This happened a lifetime ago.
Sounds ceased, owls died
but their strains adhere obdurately
to the chain of unexplained memories
that sometimes, without notice
take a swim in a warm bath of tears.

## FOR HIS PARENTS' SAKE

Racket of boots on staircase.
Commotion. Panic.

Hidden in the pantry, crouching
behind the recently made
jars of plum and apricot preserves
he heard his mother say

*They are coming to get us*
*save the boy*
*the boy must live.*

The words echoed forever in his memory.
A seven-year-old who knew he had to live.
He owed it.

In the deepest corner of his heart
in the hole agape
since they carted his mother away
those words ticked
like a disconsolate clock
reminding him of his duty
not just to live
not just, but meaningfully
despite knowing that
the hole in his heart
where grief bit into it
will not heal.

When a friend said:

*We are a damaged generation*

he resented this bitter verdict
then he asked his heart about it
and it bled.

**EPITAPH**
*To my aunts, uncles, cousins
who perished in the Holocaust*

You may have died

in the fields of poppies
crimson, guilt-flushed

in the silence of white
birch forests

in bolted trains on the way
to the camps

in the screams of
lethal showers

in the limed pits—piles of
unburied bones among bones

in your own country
in a foreign country

I don't know where or how

but this I do know:
you did not return

they've killed you all
you are gone from life

and I am not a believer
but on some clement nights

in my untamed dreams
I dare to hope your spirits will

some day mingle with mine
we will comfort each other

in the world better than this one
in the realm of undefined time

free to imagine love without loss
free to indulge in such love

## THE NIECE'S LAMENT
*For Estera*

My beautiful maiden aunt. A cascade
of raven-black hair, like my mother's.
The black eyes, now muted, look out of
a faded sepia photograph with broken edges.

A flower plucked before it fully bloomed
a young blade of grass, violently trampled
by the boots marching to a Nazi rhythm
on the path marked by the yellow star
clearly displayed. If it wasn't, the penalty
was death. Either way, the penalty was death
untimely.

Marred by a German stamp, the last mangled
postcard lied to us that you were well:
its blackened lines screamed in pain.

The time floated comfortlessly for the ones
who loved you. The sky wept disconsolate rains
wiping out the hope. The card vanished
in the flood of river Sava sent by providence
we already knew as cruel.

Why spare a postcard if the sender perished?
So did the testimony drown. And a dress that you
crocheted for me (I remember a daintiness of yarn
a gift of loving hands for a beloved niece)
also drowned.

Only a single treasure has survived:
a mere button, for that is what it is
color of pale, green grass, one of the
four buttons, each for a year of my age.

Years passed.
In a round, pink-lidded case lined with
soft, black velvet meant to hold a jewel,
the button waited. I found it, played with it.
My mother, worried I might lose it,
placed it gently back in its plushy tomb.
Omama, my grandmother, uttered misty-eyed:

*Let her play with it and hold it.*
*What are things, we have lost much more—*

I felt she wanted to say more
but words drowned in the tremble of her voice.

Both of them long gone, I became my mother
and my grandmother. I let my grandchildren
caress the treasured button's bumpy shape.

When afterwards I lay it lovingly
in its resting place of soft, black velvet
in my heart I feel connected to my dead aunt
and take comfort, such as it is.

.

So this is my lament:
that the young grass trampled by the boots
wilted, died, and vanished in the hostile soil
without a trace, and this was allowed.

And this is my sorrow:
that I remember the dress but not
your face; that I recall the softness of the yarn
but not the softness of the fingers that knitted it.

I am left with a faded sepia image
and one button, the color of pale grass
the surface of an unripe berry.

# Chapter 3

## In the Teeth of Wintry Sun

a bittersweet tune rippled
through feathers of solitude

## IN THE TEETH OF WINTRY SUN

In a room too small
odd pieces of furniture
bruise elbows and shins—

an oak bed, too large
to move to make space for day
a desk, too heavy to carry
and make space for night

a display credenza crammed
with books instead of bibelots
and floral china

a silver-sprayed furnace
too close to bed to heat
elegant
and useless in its sheen—

the signposts
of my awkward childhood
spent under things
I couldn't move nor lift

growing up with grownups
busy surviving
their worried shadows
passing over me

Outside
the icicles crackled, melting
in the teeth of wintry sun
oozing diamonds

How beautiful
days of misty breath
on the frosted windowpanes!

## HEIRLOOM

The tightly drawn shades keep the moonlight
from the center of my world.

Vague light flickers in the room;
the randomly saved furniture shabby
but oddly beautiful; a ghost of former life
hovers suspended, palpable.

We speak softly
my mother, the seamstress, and I
over the whine of scissors, clipping
cutting through a night of confidences.

Occasional gleam of stainless steel
lands on tracing paper, then slips away
and all around the table's edges
snippets fall like autumn leaves
strewn over the floor of memories.

Through the moving shadow of her bent
silhouette, the seamstress strains her gaze;
her pin-pricked, roughened fingers tend
carefully to scarce, precious cloth.

    There's no clock and no one
    observes the time.

Gently spins the treadle of an old
sewing machine, a veritable heirloom of
iron sculpted by an anonymous craftsman
leaves and tendrils wrought with tenderness.

    Listen to the hum of stitching
    a refrain of daily life.

The garment finished long ago—
scissors still, machine silent
in my arms I hold graceful forms
of wrought iron, the center of my world.

## SPLENDOR IN THE KITCHEN

Parents and child bound by

leaning walls
badly in need of repair

Father lights
a ceiling lamp

a swinging dim affair
waving puppet-shadows

Over checkered tablecloth
lay remnants of the day

some crumbs and
earthenware:

three bruised plates
three chipped tea cups

and an imitation
Delft saltshaker

They walk barefoot
The planked

splintered floor
pierces tender skin

Mother lifts the crying
child into her soft

aproned lap
kisses away the tears

*Look, darling
a banquet spread*

*the goblets
and a chandelier*

## FOR THE FAMILY LORE

The plum tree behind my house
was pruned too heavily.
In desperation, it bore fruit more profusely
the soil around it, drunk with *slivowitz*
I with memories.

*Sliva* means a plum in Croatian
the suffix *witz*, a joke in German.

I saw the face of Uncle Stephan
a born joke-teller, though he never gave
a fig for *slivovitz*—he was only a protagonist in
an annual stage production of plum jam.

Aunt Rosa stirred the fruit with special wooden
spatula carved to scrape a heavily enameled pan.
The children took turns and waited to lick it clean.

When the jam started to thicken, Uncle Stephan
solemnly delivered the same story every year.

*This is how you know the jam is done—*
*the ladle must leave a clear wake behind*
*like the hand of God when it opened a passage*
*for the ancient Jews to escape from Egypt.*

Such was the biblical lesson of the days of plums.

By the way, Uncle Stephan's name was Moses
before he changed it to be less
conspicuously Jewish. He had enough
trouble to stay alive without a name like that.

It fell to Holy Moses to part the Red Sea
it fell to his namesake to part plum jam.

The children loved the story. It found its way
into the family lore, even into this poem.

Sometimes the Bible comes alive
in the most unexpected ways.

## END OF A GRAVELLY ROAD

At the end of greening pastures
a gravelly road unravels
to a shimmering horizon.

To such an end I will unload
my arms full of flowers
fragrant fruits, pine cones.
I will lay them on the linen
embroidered with a hundred
tiny loaves of daily bread
spread over the miniature trays
I made of clay which, even when
glazed, still smells of earth—and this
will be my offering.

What I return will never be
enough—I'll always owe more

To the carpet of grass
    plush under my feet.
To the weeds I trampled but
    they didn't hurt me back.
To the plane-tree leaves
    that left me ochre melodies
    whose notes trail me faithfully
    as one constant goodness.
To the saffron-aproned daffodils
    that swayed around the gazebo
    I used to pass on my way to school.

Walking in the sun
walking in the rain.
Oh this relentless joy-sadness refrain!

I know its music by heart by now—
the notes unpredictable of living
craving, losing, loving, giving
conversation of life passing
heedless whispering of wind
rushing through the rushes
and behind the fence
the chirpy children's voices
at the end of the gravelly road.

## IN HONOR OF THE CLICHÉ: HOW TIMES HAVE CHANGED

My grandchildren's backs bend under
the backpacks crowded with books, trinkets
snacks, and an obligatory cell phone.

At their age, I carried to school a misshapen
weathered leather bag wide enough to fit
a chalkboard and a dry weightless sponge.

Growing up in Zagreb, under comrade
Tito's watchful, hammer-and-sickle eyes
it was normal not to have paper
a proof that norms can be as elastic
as chewing gum which arrived after

WWII with American care packages
in supple silver foil more precious than
chewing gum itself. Along came
cans of overly sweetened beans and spam
which no one liked, but we were hungry
and ate them gratefully.

Next to food, fancy footwear cozied up
to so much wasted tissue paper
one could cry, and we did—the shoes
too narrow for our coarsened feet.

Mothers took the shoes to cobblers:
> *Do something with them, take three pairs,*
> *four, just make me one that fits!*

The shoemaker had two daughters my age.
My mother tailored their dresses, he cobbled
our shoes for free.

I asked her:

*What would you have done
if he had no daughters?*

She replied:

*Don't be silly, I would have
thought of something else.*

She used the fabric scraps to sew skirts
as stunning as Pennsylvania Dutch quilts—
my friends and I, the mannequins, she
our Coco Chanel.

## LISTENING TO SENECA

*Solitude is for the spirit
what food is for the body.*

I paced heavily through days
of adolescence. On my shoulder

a gray stone of loneliness
veined white with threads of hope

And I was blue, and I was sad
and I was silly, and so grave

In my heart a bittersweet tune
rippled through feathers of solitude

The gray stone ached for company
the white veins did not provide any

If you have ever carried such a stone
this poem is written for you

I searched for balm in the calm
words of sages and in the faces

of passersby. I encountered eyes
which did and did not meet mine

and smiles meant for someone else
I was learning to reflect and wait

I do not know how long ago
precisely, but in its own good time

the gray stone whispered to me:
*I'm not of use to you any longer*

and in an instant fell off me
leaving a bird on my shoulder

# Chapter 4

## Figs, Hazelnuts, Muscat Grapes

and daily bread
brushed with olive oil
as was the custom of the land

## OLIVE TREE (*MASLINA*)

... I sit so calmly with a candle ...
Its oil smells like olives from my father's fields
its flame a spark of fire from the sun
and when my heart feels heavy among men
and the stormy night rages, a magic circle appears
in which, around an oil-light
my father's lovely vineyard is greening
ringed with a valance of olive trees—
below it, a boy daydreams while the grapes
ripen and the crickets sing louder and louder.
Somewhere very far, the sea gurgles and
in the clear celestial blue, there float
two clouds, slender, white ...


Excerpt from the poem "Olive Tree" (*Maslina*) by Vladimir Nazor translated from Croatian by the author.

## ISTRIA OF YORE

Figs, hazelnuts, muscat grapes

Pregnant blackberries ferment
a potent brew that cures illness
a bite of a crimson spider
a curse of an evil eye

The red land of bauxite-bitter soil
raises men in baggy jute pants
whose four-times-knotted handkerchiefs
peek like baby birds from the crumpled
straw hats whose wide rims keep
the sweat out of their eyes

At dawn, their firmly planted gait
wakes up the countryside
of their firmly planted lives

They work the tight-fisted clay;
the rusty tools of their grandfathers
fuse with the palms of their hands
until they bloom with blisters

At noon, when the tired wind subsides
and shades of silver embrace
knees of gray-green olive trees
they rest. They lean aching torsos
into gnarly tree-trunks, and from afar
the men and trees look the same

Their women carry jugs of wine
and water to dilute that which makes
heads swim in many blinding suns
spinning around scorched countryside

Ah, those girls that lilt over
meandering trails—flagons float
on top of sunshine-plated hair
For them hearts leap, the earth sways

Following the same route every day
sweeping skirts pass over the land
with tenderness—
in their path, a scent of thyme
and sweet marjoram

## THE VILLAGE MALENA

Mad Malena was on the prowl again.
She communed with wind and open sea
combed the beach for scurrying sand crabs
to seize and release, and observed them
disappear down the seeping sand.

She tamed skittish, spotted sandpipers
and confidently strutting sea gulls
but village women clung to their husbands
fearing a certain fire in her eyes—their own
glossed over with the tiredness of life.

Malena shed her smiles without discretion
and talked to grass with bare feet.
She sniffed air to remember something
or someone, and let her vague hopes
linger on the tails of an evening breeze.

She owned only a thin layer of cloth
between her skin and the rest of the world.
*Malena get dressed* the women would say
*or you will catch your death of cold.*

Malena would shake her wild curls in reply
and stare ahead with those charcoal eyes
which could burn a hole in the driftwood
the sea left her on the beach each night.

In those days, they wouldn't lock you up
for being Malena. She passed by the native
medicinal plants and didn't gather any, but
she garnered armfuls of thorny, wild roses.

An old woman wrapped a white kerchief
around her bleeding fingers, saying kindly:
*Malena, be more careful next time* and
offered her food which Malena snatched
though it was a gift, hid it underneath

her single-layer dress, fled to the beach
and tossed the roses into the rolling sea.
She went to sleep under a laurel tree
spilling hair over the pillow of driftwood.

## A BLUE FAN

Wheels played rumba on the tracks:
bah-rumba, bah-rumba, rumba.

Thirteen and on vacation
a notebook of empty pages
a face leaning out the window
the wind dwindling in my hair.

The sea appeared from nowhere:
an inverted triangle of azure
just a slit of it at first
then a large blue fan exploded
into an aquamarine shimmer
that wounded me.

No other sea could be so lovely!
It colored my longings blue
scented them with salt.

Slowly and deliberately
the train glided into Rovinj
leaving the view behind.

All my life I searched for that
blue fan in different oceans.
I made my own private waves
smashed them into a thousand gems
gazed into eyes of cobalt
spellbinding but false.

I pondered a trembling tide pool
trapped by the receding sea—
a school of silver specks
too warm for their scaly habits
swarmed and waited for a swell
to take them home.

I waited with them. I still wait—
past all tides I wait for water
to wear the right shade of blue.
It never does. It never will
but my bewitched heart obeys
the spell of the blue fan.

## A WAR WIDOW
*To Foshka*

Framed by a leaning doorway
a black obscuring dress engulfs
a small figure still upright and slender.

A delicate face in a wreath of pewter
wrinkled by the merciless sun
and more merciless grief:
a capsule of living gone by
like her irretrievable husband.

Cornflower eyes peer uncomplaining
slightly astonished at the way of life.

I know this woman.

She is an aroma of home. A smell of baked bread
and ripe peaches, a terracotta floor mopped clean
intimate articles airing on the homespun cord
summer heat streaming through ill-fitting shutters
a memory of forgotten apples wafting from the cellar.

She speaks through the whispers of half-empty rooms
squeaking chairs, dripping faucets
and barely audible cats' paws
shuffling to the scraps she leaves them
God's poor creatures.

She is the fading of a day into a night
mourning dress laid out for the grief-muted
sunrises that lie ahead.
She is all that.

A wife that kept a vigil by her lifeless husband
brought to her one balmy night when the moon turned dull
and stars stopped shining shamed by their splendor.

A mother who beheld her children flee
the impoverished nest
as the fog grew over lingering footprints.

She is that, too.

Once she was comely.
Grace trailed her like a bridal train.
Laughter crowned her home as the foam
crowns the waves of effervescent ocean.
Her loveliness was everywhere.

## SUNDAY BREAD

Down at the bottom of hilly old town
where sprawling houses sprout like underbrush
around aging trees, a row of chimneys broke
the harmony of terracotta roof tiles: a bakery
without name or number, for none were needed
enveloped in leavened aroma
of fresh bread and Sunday dainties.

There Doro lived alone, a happy simple-minded man
never called by the name his mother gave him:
Teodoro, a gift of God, her beautiful baby.

As he grew, he learned to bake bread; he clung
to his aprons and his new name, and felt safe.

He held a daily race with dawn: brought in the wood
and stoked the fire, fanned it with leather bellows
waited for pious womenfolk in their Sunday best;
as they lifted white linen off their wicker baskets
and recommended the braids of dough to his care
they smiled at him, and he knew he was beloved.

As elegantly as a maestro conducting legato, he swept
the bulging loaves of bread onto oval trays, and with
a long, charred handle shoved them deep into the
oven's glowing heart. He performed this ritual until
the last black skirt turned the corner on its way to church—
a blackbird flown away through early morning fog.

Unadorned and small, the church was a rest
from steep steps of stone worn out by devotion
a holy place where women kneeled with covered
heads, spilling their hearts out to favorite saints
then warbled down the steps, while shadows receded
chastened by the purified morning.

Bread was timed to bake very slowly, to be
ready for women returning from morning mass.

Flushed from the heat of the oven Doro proudly waited
his face shiny as the daily bread brushed with
olive oil, as was the custom of the land.

The women took the wicker baskets back to
Sunday tables to infuse their various joys and
troubles with the comfort of freshly baked bread.

# Chapter 5

## Love, What Else?

such as we
two pieces of a puzzle

**CONUNDRUM**

How details fade
in the distance of reflective hills
How essence crystalizes

Loss and gain

Locked in an endless dance
an action and reaction
balance and rule the world

But what rules the heart?

## A LOVE SONG

In the silence of the sleeping house
I reach to you across the damask sheet
I ironed in my domesticity. I tap
the warmth of your beloved hand
the unaware anchor of my soul
so close, so far away in slumber.

How did I find you in the vast mosaic
of encounters, recognize you, hold you
with confidence older than my age?
How did I know to follow love, let
your hand lead mine in complete trust?

Such as we, two pieces of a puzzle
intimately fit and feel each other's shape.

>   The two parallel tracks
>   carrying the train of life.

Waking up affectionate, together
we remembered the night's joyful secrets
we wove our days with yarn of work
of hope and of laughter.

Our children,
the proof of us in their features
and in their children's, carry traits
by that same train through generations
recognizable just now and then
in posture or in voice
in the way a smile enters the face
or by chance, in a thought unregistered
owned previously by some ancestor.

Thus nature's own
awarding harvest.

Trying was the ride at times
balancing the happiness with sadness
but for all the bafflement of life
our hands stayed intertwined
in tender motivation.

The days strung an open necklace.
The unfailing seasons streamed by
unaccounted for and we, too absorbed
in living to ponder their preciousness
did not notice the passing.

The train slows down approaching
the destination; absurdly, time gathers
speed flowing towards a halting age
but the spell that led me through life
remains unharmed. I still heed its call.

## ORLANDO
*In homage to Virginia Woolf*

On a remote promontory
on the other side of
time and space I wait for you

Above me the wild geese
streak immense emptiness

and at my feet, a dust of dusk
hesitates to settle down

Alone in a crowd, I look for you
amid a swirl of faces

who with their noisy purpose
point to my loneliness

Someday I will find you as naturally
as a drop of water falls when it's full

as an amplitude of one bird's song
reaches another

and awakened earth lays a carpet
of the season's gifts

plush in their greening mantles
ripe in sultry, luxurious scent

Our souls will blend then
in a single burst of recognition

mute but eloquent
receiving and giving

until all opposites appeased
rest on the smoothness of a lagoon

## CRESCENDO

I am drunk on sunshine
trapped between the golden skin

and luscious flesh of grapes
fermented in the darkness of a wooden
barrel girdled with iron rings belted in flames

I am inebriated by the sound of
crickets chirping unceasingly, strumming
pizzicato on violin-limbs, charmed by their own love call

Above all, my beloved,
I am enamored of you. Retire now
you superfluous moon——we don't desire
your radiance tonight, only the flickering of ardent fireflies

## JOY

In darkness
Spider webs glitter
Suspended in delicacy

Keen buds wait to open
Urgently pressing on slim
Young branches of sugar plum

How nature palpitates with joy!
You, my heart, now join this night
Of young passion, a humid night of love

Bodies speak, skin to receiving skin
Souls reveal themselves in a touch

## NASTURTIUM DREAMS

In reality

we are together

In dreams

each in one's own

Yet in the budding light of this morning

I remember having dreamt of us

treading the same path

in parallel steps

and the path was merry

with nasturtiums

and the air scented

with honeysuckle

❀ ❀ ❀

You sleep so peacefully next to me

If I wake you up now

would you

could you

remember us

being together

in my dream?

## PORTRAIT OF BAKA
*for my mother*

Snuggled in a woolen shawl
On a wooden spool
Rocking chair
A halo of wispy white hair
Rested on the subtly heaving breaths
Of her sunken chest

She offered her palms
To balmy summer air
And everywhere
Sounds relented

The breeze ceased
The rocking chair calmed
The sun bent down
Kissed her shoulders
Took her by the hand
Opened a dreamy gate

A book slipped from her lap
And fell asleep in a crib of daisies

# Chapter 6

## The Roots of Things

*their desperate hands came
from far away*

**BITTER HERBS**

Mother, I don't like the bitter herbs
those you gather bending in the scrub.

> Eat your supper, son!
> Rutabaga, radicchio, and turnips are
> alms of this unyielding land.
>
> They drink of the mountain brook
> that unfolds past the great oak
> in whose shade primroses
>
> and their cousins, cowslips
> made a bed for you and brushed
> your sleeping brows with sweetness.

But Mother
I don't like the taste of wild herbs.
I'll look tomorrow for different pastures.

> Yes, I know, my son.
> Have your supper.
> Stay the night.
>
> Tomorrow, you'll give your
> thanks to the great oak
> and I will not hold you back.

## FOLLOWING A RAINBOW

Glitter of allure
twinkles in air—
a glass stairway
I know not to where
until I mount it

Crystal slippers
wrought of hope
ring delicate bells
Oblivious to fear
I follow the rainbow

Blinding is the light
slippery the stairway
I do not know
what to search for
but what I find
will be beautiful

## IN THE SPACE OF FANTASY

Borderless, mauled
by waves

which rolled me
I shed my soul

like old fence
about to fall

Now that I know
who I am not—

no tribe or belief
will ever own me

I shall bounce again
on dry land

and draw
the strength

from simplicity of
a wild trillium

My eyes will swim
in wonderment

that there may be
so much power

in a minimal
arrangement

of a simple flower
tiny in the space of fantasy

## A TALE OF TRASTEVERE

Two thousand years ago and some
fine rain sprinkled our fellow Romans.
It's lovely to get wet by spring rain:
then, just like now, young skin perked
eyes sparkled behind dark eyelashes
the air heady with violets when boys offered
shelter to girls and received more.

Fifty years ago and some,
huddled under a new umbrella, we spoke
tender words to each other
lover to lover—delicious, silly words
like a mother whispering to a child

In Trastevere in Rome
the river Tiber swelling
and we, safe behind
the curtain of bouncing raindrops
poor but free at last
walking ahead, alone-together
in a perfume of violets.

How the time slowed down
for the two of us lost in the rain!

Fifty years later and some
back in Trastevere
nestled again in the hum
of autumn rain—
we say fondly
in our husky voices
*come closer, don't get wet
you may catch a cold.*

Now that we are old, we pause
lean over the railing
walk some more and listen
to the Water Music
playing on our umbrella.

## IMMIGRANT SILVER

In the silverware drawer rests a set
of six old knives, odd and dated

Handles faux-wood, chocolate-brown
grooves worn smooth, blades tarnished
but always meticulously scrubbed

Grown up children wonder at such
shabby utensils but the parents revere
them and do not feel a need
to defend their fondness

They recall the ship called *Independence*

How it glided, a confident white swan
into the port of New York in sight of
the Green Lady, her alluring drapes
barely discernible in early morning fog

With hope in their pockets, they were
better off than many, having brought along
a certain independence
that comes from having a profession

They worked hard. When they filled the car
with liquid fumes that smelled like success
the Shell station gifted them a knife
until they had a collection of artifacts
grooved with memories of aspirations
more dear than achievements

They can never dispose of them any more than
they can throw away the memory of their youth

## THE ROOTS OF THINGS

I was digging up the soil
for the fledgeling plants

When some thirsty roots appeared
from parched lands

Their desperate hands
came from far away

Those trailblazing immigrants
Nature's entrepreneurs

Like beggars they arrived
from underground

Haggard and deprived
singing an ode to hope

I dug around them tenderly
quivering with empathy

One doesn't always know
where life may linger trying to survive

One doesn't always know
one's self

# Chapter 7

## Letting Go

there goes the past
here comes the future

**FUGUE**

A cloud
    dreamy
        silvery

I climb it
    to be myself
        in the realm
            of my own

When called down to life
feet firm on the ground
around the family dinner table
surrounded by dear faces

I still long
    to climb
        to that other life
            on the cloud
                on my own

## WALKING IN BELMONT

Cornered by a string of modest ranches in the patches
of sage and rosemary, yucca and purple penstemon
an English Tudor house oddly impresses indeed.

Staged as it is in the garden in which rain fairies
live in sprinklers, it maintains the illusion of lushness
in this arid land.

Tradition intertwines with ivy
climbing up the decorative beams
while manicured lawn speaks fondly of flowered hats
such as English queens wear at ceremonies
and that southern beauties wore to debutante balls.

I say to myself: *there goes the past.*

A couple saunters by.
She, draped in a crimson sari
    what could her husband do but love her
    so enveloped in billowing grace.
He, in his longings colored red and orange
    hears the whisper of a tamarind tree.

I keep walking.
A young boy's round face
peers out of a slow moving car.
He smiles at me with all of his seven or eight years
of beaming friendliness.

In the Carlmont Plaza
a swarm of high school students
all colors, fashions, and voices
perch on the stools of outdoor cafes
chattering like birds on telephone wires
enjoying their integrated lunch.

They don't know yet what they are about—
their eyes shine with adolescent eagerness of life
that hasn't written much into their faces yet.

I say to myself: *here comes the future.*

## LETTING GO

Gleaming in the sun, a white
picket fence frames the fragrant
spread of freshly mowed grass
trampled by children—a playground
of young things wriggling around
in damp sand, building mounds
molding them, calling them castles
and two baby swings, occupied.

> *High, high, up to the sky*
> *Johnny will fly, Johnny will fly.*

A young mother swings her baby
rosy cheeks and sparkling eyes
all things budding and tender—
vigorous swings paving the rest
of the day, the rest of the week
urged on by gurgles of joy
calling for more, more, more.

A three-year-old squirms
wriggles out of his mother's clasp
whooshing down the precarious slide
meant for an older child.

> *By myself, by myself!*

This is where the fugue begins:
on this freshly mowed lawn, on
the swing of memories of letting go.

Another woman, older and foreign
swings someone else's precious
up and down, up and down.

She misses the rosy cheeks and
sparkling eyes of her children
nieces, nephews, too many, too dear
her heart left behind with her native sun
whose burning breath melted the clay
of her abandoned hearth.

Her eyes on her charge gloss over.
She remembers with aching sweetness
the small shapes growing smaller
as the distance pebbled with the unexpected
weighed down her arms
anchored her ankles with worry.

What will the future allow?

The sun climbs up
the invisible ladder without an answer.
It is lunchtime; the players leave
this lovely stretch of grass framed
by the white picket fence
and the song that plays itself out
over and over again.

## THE MIMOSA ON AVON STREET

A hundred eyes bored through my back—
    the gaping knots were staring at me
    from the trunk of a mimosa tree
    bare but for a few precocious buds
    sparsely dotting its denuded skin.

The gaping knots were staring at me
    through the scars implanted in the bark
    that marked a special kind of loss:
    perhaps of some aborted twigs
    or an axe's mutilation of the limbs.

With the scars implanted in the bark
    the tree imposed on me its sadness
    it resembled nature's rendering
    of a Magritte painting, but more
    sinister, alive and darkly insistent.

The tree imposed on me its sadness—
    I tried to recall its previous splendor
    but could not—the nagging impression
    having left my eyes, has already
    settled deeper. Again, fervently

I tried to recall its previous splendor
    hoping the tree will bloom again
    despite its wounds, and the golden
    clusters of velvety tufts will be
    oblivious to the pain that bore them.

I hope the tree will bloom again
    and bask rejuvenated in the sun.
        Come, walk with me down Avon Street!
        Together, we'll soon forget the wounds
        and celebrate the coming of spring.

## TERRACE AFTER THE RAIN

You would think the terrace in my garden ordinary
but today you would be wrong.

The rain has stopped.
Across the relieved skies
the wind chases the fugitive clouds.
The sunshine, released
spills its rays triumphantly
through live oak trees.

On the ground
a breeze brushes over
the puddles gleaming in all stages of glitter
from discreet to jubilant—
falling leaves dance, delicate shadows
weave a restless lace
on the mirror below.

The birds have joined in the celebration
darting from branches to eaves
so eagerly
so swiftly
that seconds after they vanish
only their speed is left behind.

They twitter and bicker
in sheer exuberance
of air cleansed by rain.
They survey the scene
for careless worms lounging in wetness
then swoop down to harvest the bounty.

Under their wings
the crinkled leaves shiver—
branches spring
free from their small weights
like bowstrings from arrows
they vibrate and sprinkle more raindrops.

Tomorrow, beautiful Siena will come
and draw on gray slate
the white lines of hopsotch
a sun with yellow tresses, squiggly and
splendid as a lion's mane and some
children's faces to keep her company.

Racing up the trees
the squirrels will stop
observe her design
and too shy to join her
chatter in admiration.

She will be glad to have her easel dry again
but I long for those fallen leaves
to repeat their country dance on my wet terrace.

## A VISIT TO PALY HIGH SCHOOL

The door to the classroom was ajar
I pushed it open, entered a new world

In front of me a medley of students—
the shades of
    pale moon
        white porcelain
            mahogany
                ebony

a blessed spread of colors as created
before ugly words like
    differentness
        and foreignness
            were ever invented

From the tilt of my granddaughter's head
stray curls escaped
    unruly
        springy
            ready to move with wind—

lanky limbs
taut heels impatient
    set to lift off the flat ground
        to sprint, span
            the earth, make it
                a home for everyone

She was one among others
as similar to them as if related
a body of hope advancing
one eager wave of youth

Salty-sweet drops pooled in my eyes
Driving home I took my time—the steering
wheel held up my arms, drove on its own
while I embraced the world in gratitude

# Chapter 8

## Ultimate Nightmare

a mad dramaturge out of ideas
calls for a monkey to man the machine

**CRUEL DAWN**
*November 9th, 2016*

I peel myself
out of myself, compelled
to remember last night

Barely out of a deep sleep
I do not see but only feel
the nascent morning coming

I tremble and crave to
crawl back to the frame
of a lightless snail shell

and let things stay
the way they were
day before yesterday

Oh dreams, come back
and carry away
this cruel dawn

## ULTIMATE NIGHTMARE

An odd scenario emerges from darkness
a phantasmagoria of sinister shapes.
Silence slides insidiously into noise
grumbling, growing, exploding.

The upheaval shatters the old mold—
the new one, forged in agony
of great anguish and ideals
pleasing to some, odious to others—
its final appearance uncertain
but the clay stays always the same.

This is the orchestra of fate or evolution
violent and fecund at the same time—
the well-oiled machinery broken
the faulty design replaced often
fails a delicate, patched-up balance
in some weak, obscure spot.

A proverbial straw. A spaghetti-bowl of
entangled software, strangled by itself.

A vision of more revolutions overwhelms
until all scenarios are reenacted—
a mad dramaturge, out of ideas, calls
for a monkey to man the machine.

The monkey pushes the button:
a roughly spun skirt wins over a crinoline
a spade hits flesh instead of earth
ferries carry loads of heavy water
meant for someone else, and drones
spread the final, intended pollution.

Of such stuff, nightmares are made
which abort the day.

Oh my heart, do not yield
to the horrors of the night
banish fears even when justified.
Feed not on despair but on hope
or you'll be suffocated by the mind
before your time.

## A MISSING INSTRUMENT

A family starts the morning while
the media in the background
promote healthy eating habits:

*A portion of salmon served frequently ...*
and on and on ... One's longevity
exchanged for another's.

Complacency oozes out of
the king salmon's scales as
the irony of it startles his gills:
water flows, there is no death
only change in this world
     of hunters and the hunted.

Thousands of moons ago, the native
sons revered the bounty by singing
to it through the slap of oars
upon the ocean, as they prayed
     to nature to forgive
     the killing for sustenance.

Thousands of moons ago, the drums
beat a sacred song of expiation
and the song was pleasing to the gods.
     But that was then.

Now the king is crowned
with the wreath of nets cast
in the spirit of impunity.
Some day a folk singer will chant
     at the royal funeral.

He alone will shed a tear
for an instrument missing from
the vast orchestra of wilderness
while the good earth will ache
burdened with too many of us
    and our follies.

But eternal time, as always
will soothe and smooth all.
Life flows. Even death is
    only a change.

## A GLIMMER OF HOPE

In this pitch-black night, I suffocate
in the hold of a loud, threatening cloud
of lawyers' gowns swishing in arguments

and politicians plotting and scheming.
The heavy hand of time presses on my shoulder.
A storm is gathering, the simple folk despairing.

Stop squabbling you rulers, rich, mighty and crafty!
Heed the seething mob below; can you not
foresee an avalanche of anger rising
out of those numberless, nameless shoulders?

Shudder cushioned lives! Rewrite yourselves
you books of right and wrong—this ferment
doesn't know of rules. Fear, you are justified

to fill the hearts, make them race like rabbits.
The horses will un-domesticate themselves
the bisons stampede over desiccated earth

and let no child's cradle be in their way
for accidents know not of guilt.
Oh Eisenstein, we need you now to record
the silent screams before they are audible.

Our nostrils, stunned obtuse by the good life,
cannot smell anything—not the spreading fires
not even the stench of dead sea-lions washed ashore

on the petroleum-spilled, black-tarred beaches.
Numbed numb, how can we detect an odorless
annihilation threat?

It is almost morning.
The light is seeping sheepishly into my room.
Shaken by a nightmare—is that what it was?
I dread to hear the news, listen to bewildered
grownups already resigned or about to resign.

This time, it will take the youth to lift the world
out of its demise. I will look for answers in my
grandchildren's faces—how I long to see
sparks of elan in their clear, scintillating eyes

a determination settle in the stubborn jawlines.
I will listen to their naive but sincere political
arguments, watch the future brighten in
youthful expressions. I think they will ripen well.

In them, only, do I see the light.

## WANTON WORDS
*After Robert Frost's "Mending Wall"*

*Something there is that doesn't love a wall.*
Built *to please the yelping dogs* in love
with boundaries, defenders of gaps
rivers without bridges, uncrossable
festering, noxious differences.

Abroad, in the least likely place
aboard a small cruise ship, I found the Wall.
A neighbor who leaned across the table, bawled:

> I miss my trusty pistol. It was too much trouble
> to check it in, you know. The boulders they throw
> in our freedom way! I don't feel safe today.

> Why do you need to carry a pistol every day?

> I carry it because I like it! And I also like the Wall!

Oh Wanton Words, Wasps in my ears
hissing Wayward, Wrong, and Wangling sin!
Wall is a new four-letter word.

The Wall of China, the Berlin Wall, Our Wall—
how many Walls of Wicked Waste must be?
By many degrees, the Wall of Robert Frost is
a pale ghost of Our Wall, an affront to all.

Something there is, that must hate the Wall.

# Chapter 9

## Of Different Strengths

what of those who know their strength
and refuse to play the game?

## DANCING ON A SPIDER WEB

To be entranced!
To imbibe the morning dew
that night, overflowing with tenderness
exhaled upon sleepy leaves!

A mad ballerina possessed by her slippers
I will dance on balance beams of a spider web
Shimmering filaments will receive me with a deceptive fragility

Out of pity they will welcome me
a devil-daring guest, and my weight. I will be the envy
of a dainty dragonfly, whose wings, however marvelously veined

are dipped in the blue milk of fear. He is
not my rival, for I am brave in my brazenness.
To dance! To dance and to deceive myself!

## WEB IN A BRAVE NEW WORLD

No, not a spider web
a computer web
the one entrapping men
who seek instant knowledge
surfing tenaciously.

No, not with a surfboard
with a little mouse
not one that squeaks
but one that clicks and looks
like a large plastic lady bug
that ran out of red ink
and lost its polka dots.

Black or white
to fit the room decor
this tireless magic wand
conjures up screens.

No, not real screens
the virtual ones, although
both fulfill their original purpose
which is to screen off
the intruding world.

Over the keyboard similar
to a stunted piano
with black alphabetic keys
busy fingers stray to bring
additional screens.

In this inevitable world
worlds instantly change
at the motion of a hand.
The rigid pages flicker
under every touch
but unlike book pages
don't feed the senses.

More and more I miss that
difficult, passé world of ours
in which a great effort was
needed to learn a little
but in whose natural order

flowers smelled, bees hummed
and children read books
long past their bedtime
with an old-fashioned flashlight
cozy under the covers.

## OF DIFFERENT STRENGTHS

You board it only once
The merry-go-round starts
slowly, then spins out

Hold onto the rail you must
or drop to the side
be dragged behind

Have you lost your nerve?
Not enough speed
not enough verve

to lift your face, ignore
the bruises on your hands
Get up, challenge, fight!

Living is for the strong
move over, weaklings
go pick the daisies!

The world bows to a winner
It does not revere
inner victories

But what of those who know
their strength and refuse
to play the game?

In the realm of flowers
the ducats are not beautiful
but to see that
one must walk the meadow

## CALM AFTER THE STORM

I am the surface of the water and stir easily.
Gentle breezes ruffle me just enough
to fan a net of jolly wrinkles all over my belly.
I absorb the balmy vibrations and save them
gratefully in a chamber where happiness dwells.

But when wind gets rough and beats with fists
upon my tenderness I hold onto immovable cliffs.
Fear steels me against the punishment
of thrashing waves, while opaque survival pearls
glitter faintly under sunken skiffs.

The storm will pass for those who endure
as storms must, and when the calm returns
the waters I have protected will again repose
undisturbed in the depths, while I tend to
my bruises and become deliciously smooth.

A child will skip a stone over me to observe
the silvery ripples grow and dissolve, and I will lay
the precious token next to my pearls and cherish it.

When night falls, a golden moon will descend
from the sky on a silken ladder, and swim inside me.

.

## AT THE EDGE OF IRONY

I blend all of you Sibyls into one
as I hear peals of your laughter
reverberate through centuries.

How you made the syntax fool the lovers
and statesmen alike, so they heard what
they wanted to hear! How the kingdoms
collapsed by a misinterpreted oracle!

By the play of mighty words, so fragile
by allure of beautiful Helen, by the promise
that pervades the freshly plowed fields
and by anything that brushes our living skin
with a faintest touch, we blunder through
this world of ours held by the invisible powers.

It is irony that really presides—
a broken silence starts an avalanche
a chance that by accumulation wins
as we strive for most and the biggest
and designs flounder and die
of their own grandeur.

When the curtain falls it all comes to

    how well we live, every day,
    and how well we live every day;

    how much we love, every day,
    and how much we love every day.

The choice is ours but for a spider web!

Leave me, Sibyl, I'm done.

With wax I will fill my ears as I pass you by
a ship sailing through the night, navigating
by the stars, a blind man listening to his cane.

# Chapter 10

## A Spread of Wings

feathers welded by
wax and hope

## LOFTY ON THE HORIZON

To love
create
give
is to live
and it should suffice

but my dreams are woven
with a different weave

they entice every nerve
to be a string on a guitar

inviting me
to give myself to joy
frolic like a leaf
being tossed about

to dance a slow dance
to a murmur of a serpentine river
snaking through a meadow
of lustrous yellow
buttercups and
purple irises

to inhale
pale grandeur
of mountains
lofty on the horizon

## THE WHITE KNEE SOCKS

I have traveled many places
blending differences
of languages and garments
until I came home.

I schooled my thoughts:
the bits and the bytes
cycled in my brain
congesting it with
hexadecimal games
that write codes
that drive machines
into a loopy
technological frenzy.

I drove cars in more or less
proscribed speeds
and myself
within my limits
on some very crowded
some very lonely roads.

I have a family: a husband
children and grandchildren—
I try to think on their level
they meet me on mine
as befits the pawns in this
venerable, ancient game.

I have lived my life, although
it seems at times more likely
that life has lived through me

but when I look inside
a little girl in white knee socks
looks back at me.

## SANTORINI

A fathomless sea
of the bluest of lapis lazuli
leans on the haze of horizon

Against this magnificent spread
all shapes measure themselves
all colors shimmer in awe

A *fata morgana*—
the cliffs of caldera emerge
from the Aegean sea

a phoenix, still trembling
submerged for too long
a white dove, released

Oh Santorini of azure domes
and whitewashed houses
framed by undiluted sienna

and green and blue!
And above
more blue

Men and women live
under your kind auspices
carrying in their souls

names of ancient gods
in ancient alphabet
engraved in broken marble

They teach children the glory
that was Greece, and let
their everyday lives

melt in a liquid landscape
Like dots in a busy design
resident ants mill on

a sandy beach and slowly
disappear in the spread
of the white island floating

on the sea of blue
From a cloudless sky
the benevolent sun

blazes and caresses
the infinite lover
radiating life

## ICARUS

Feathers welded by
wax and hope

Who shall I be
Earth Mother, what shall I do?
Shall I fly high

or stay close to you
to graze on the cornucopia
of your generosity?

A chameleon alters color
his courage swiveling
on the seesaw of circumstances

Endowed with steady nature
mouse scurries
eagle flies

but man waxes flexible
until the rubber band breaks
without warning

Sunflower to sun
I turn to chance—
a mauve path beckons

from the bridge
suspended over
a bluff of the unknown

If I embark on it
the clouds will part
The mouse will know

nothing of this
but the eagle
will welcome me

## KAPNIKAREA

Sound of ages, remnant of centuries.
Meaning of your name, buried in a shroud of time.

A church. A surprise, stolidly squatting
between the shading modern city blocks
      the three-story high tunnels of commotion
      luring the man-bees into the man-hives
      buzzing, rushing, searching
      scrambling for the slice of now.

Enthroned in the square, left you
as if out of respect
      an island of loveliness
      in the maze of whirling life
      you wear your cloak of stones
      with utter indifference.

Beware those who enter by an arched, mosaic-adorned
portal into an unlit interior;
you may never leave the same.

Darkness parts reluctantly—
through clumsy, obscuring scaffolding, byzantine
gold-littered saints bestow awe on intruders.

So powerful are those bearded images
yet so fragile, corroded slowly by black mold
forcing its seeping greed upon the helpless forms
bound by eloquent silence, secretive.

I hear an echo of wars fought long ago:
    horses neighing, irreverence interrupting
    sacred rituals, cacophony of destruction
    clash of cultures writing in vain
    history pages for future generations.

Oh, Kapnikarea
No more restoration. Allow the fade into dignity.

My soul flutters having witnessed your distress
while you stand there implacable and persevere.

I'll never again walk under your secured arches
never see your restored frescoes, never meet
tourists gawking at your newly coated splendor.

Time, an insidious spider, will spin
an unforgiving web between us.
New impressions will claim space
but I will never forget you.

You'll beckon to me from afar and I will hear
tolling of bells reverberating
from your staggered rooftops:

It is I:
KAP NI KAREA

**FADO**

The moon sailed a quarter of its heavenly route.
In taverns of cavernous Lisbon, past a late repast
Men and women sway to the plaintive sound of fado.

A woman is belting out a song, hoarse with longing
For an unshackled past, for scattered lovers and all
That is gone and will be mourned.

Another voice unwinds from the coils of smoke—
Young or old, it matters not—it unleashes the soul
And reaches to another until they ache together.

Music spills on *azulejos* of the trembling streets.
Lights flicker in sympathy and a stray passerby
Pauses spellbound in ruptured loneliness.

Fado, fa do. Fate.
Sailors drift at sea dreaming of lost loves
A luminous moon, a starry tapestry.

# Chapter 11

## Bending Boundaries

I want to be a field
without a fence

**SUBLIMINAL**

A sentence
A syllable

I stand still
statue-still

garnering
what's left of it—

a taste
in my mouth

a liquid feeling

in the shape of
a windowsill

without
a window

Pure Magritte

## STAY UNRESOLVED AND I WILL LOVE YOU

De Chirico, Ernst, Dali, and Magritte
I like that you don't spell things out, allowing me
to fantasize, to brood—what does it all mean?
and let my diverse feelings whirl unimpeded
about your whimsical, uncharted wheels!

Today I react to you thus and so
another time, not at all! But always
the freedom from having to understand
and from boredom.

My dear Magritte, I choose you today.
I put on your black bowler hat and eat of
your green apple which enables everything—
flight from obligation
escape to imagination
thrill of the unresolved.

Tomorrow I may let De Chirico birds fly
and awaken those antique marble bodies
strewn around like so many dead stones
which they are not really, but are alive
with possibilities in these
licentious landscapes
that confuse the physical and the imaginary
without censure, which is the delight of them.

And if I ascend with you, my Dali
take me to new time zones of watches
which melt and drip
and I will send sun rays
to reflect on them and change their silhouettes.
I will stop a brook from flowing, just like you
I will make the impossible real, as long as you
allow me to inhabit your canvases.

But with you, Ernst and your birds of flaming colors
which speak the unspeakable of raw feelings
I am shy. I need their boldness. I welcome them.
Please come in.
Meet your pupil.
I want to be a field without a fence.
Teach me but beware! Do not tell me everything.
Let me keep my inquisitive wings and I will love you.

## BENDING BOUNDARIES

I speak in different tongues. I also think in different tongues
    but the choice is not always mine, and that is the rub.
    Thoughts come and go in Croatian or English—if they
    appear in the wrong form, the insistent little devils
    I have a heart-to-heart talk with them and dismiss them.

When I stroll through the familiar speech-forest of my youth
    the word-flowers glitter in shade of sentences, discreet
    comely, scented with incense, sized for a small child's hand.
    The smell of tiny, crimson cyclamen reminds me of my
    school backpack jammed with lost, uncultivated days.

I pluck flowers from the forest floor and play with them
    like I would with toys—rules of the game in my bones.
    The grammar, the syntax, the murmur of the brook
    hop into a humble nosegay to be brought home and
    kept in a breakfast cup for as long as they will last.

At the edge of the forest, a view opens an English meadow:
    a rainbow of choices, bountiful, confusing, seducing array
    of orange poppies, agapanthus, orchids, bent on forming
    my thoughts to conform to their grammar, their syntax.
    I bind them into a lavish bouquet fit for a porcelain vase.

The forest fringe frays.
    The words wander more and more often from
    one world to another, bending boundaries. In the end
    they will riot together—until I lose myself in them
    and find my Self.

I don't know yet what will be the form of the last word.

## THE VAGARIES OF CONSONANTS

It's a joy but also a five-aspirin headache to speak
in foreign tongues. To those of us who come to the U.S.
after a certain age of about sixteen, an accent will cling
forever and be charming or annoying. So one
must jump as high as one can to clear the hurdles
of pronunciation.

Remember the **GHT** of *nighty-night* and *naughty*
and the **GH** in *laugh* and the **LF** in *half*?

I could also make a case for the coupling
of the letters **T** and **H**—the lispy **TH** you hear
in *thistle, thunder,* and *through thick and thin*
or the raspy **TH** in *this,* and *that,* and *there*
but I would *rather not bother*. It would be easier
to count the stars in the luminous Tahiti skies.

Instead, I'll stake my take on the **C** and **H**—I'll reign in
those *chalky chains of chance, choose my champs*
play a game of *chess* or *checkers* with the *cheeky child
chasing Choo-Choo* trains and spunky *chipmunks.*

Just as I thought I got it, the **C** and **H** bonded
whispered mischievously, came up with the sound
of **SH** and bequeathed it to a *chanteuse* and
a *chauffeur*. I know English honored French who
got there first, but why is *Chicago* not pronounced
with a hard **CH** like *chicken*? I don't understand. It's fine
for *charlatans* to guess—but I need to know for sure.
Incidentally, the word *sure*, should for sure, according to me
be spelled with **S-H-U-R-E**.

Back to **CH** that pretends to be **SH**: what a lovely SH
I hear in a *chandelier*, *chateau*, and *chivalry*, but what
an ugly one in *chauvinism* that has recently been
gaining momentum.

Personally, rather than to stick to any "ism"
I prefer to drink *champagne* and be *chic* but never *chichi*.

As my guessing chances approach fifty-fifty, I should
remember—Beware of Greeks bearing language gifts:
a **CH** masquerading as a **K** that takes shelter
in the *character* of a *chimera*
and in the hopefulness of *chrysalis*.

Formerly, such combinations were Greek to me
to paraphrase the Irish monks who knew no Greek
yet labored to translate ancient texts, saving the
civilization from *chaos* and cessation.

About *chaos*: we proceeded from it
but would just as soon not end by it.

About cessation: I won't mention a sweet farce
known as *Chlorine* and *Chloroquine*.

I think I drove the point in. I humbly beg your pardon
but for the pain those cluster-consonants have caused me
I need to have some fun, stay *chipper*, *chortle* a little
as I *cheerfully* confess, I know full well, it took
audacity to write this poem!

Why, it took *chutzpah*! Trust a Yiddish word to clinch
a **CH**, trip one up, donate yet another variant:
the sound of an **H** that coughs as hard as a drum.

*Chutzpah* means to have a nerve or gall, such as mine.
But since this word now resides in the Webster's
English dictionary—it's legal even though it's pronounced
almost like an **H** in *holy* and *humdrum*.

Yeah, come to think of it, this poem took a lot of *chutzpah*.

## THE POETRY OF DECIMAL NUMBERS

Zero is for absence, powerless
    in its elliptical nothingness
    too arid to nurture, and like
    a secret, long undiscovered.

One is for the beginning, a solo
    braving the world with originality
    lonely treading untravelled paths.

Two is for a couple
    two pairs of eyes and hands and
    hope that sustains them.

Three is for a triangle
    the least number of lines that form
    an elemental plan figure;
    man, woman and child
    the three primary colors embracing.

Four is for that lucky leaf of clover
    hosting an extra petal;
    also for harmony, for in it
    $2 + 2$ and $2 \times 2$ join
    in exquisite symmetry.

Five is for the simplicity of a pencilled star
    drawn by a hand of a small child
    and for the beauty of cinquefoil.

Six is for the number of days
    in which the world was created
    in a story like a fairy tale.

Seven is for the dwarves
    who sing 'hi-ho' and live
    in the hearts of children.

Eight is for an octave
    danced upon by elegant fingers
    for a small, reclining sign of infinity
    and for figure-eights traced by
    a skillful skater over sparkling ice.

Nine is for long months of waiting
    for new life, and for the
    Nine Muses who inspire miracles.

Ten is not a number but an impostor
    who combines beginning with nothingness:
    a blueprint to generate new orders
    which spin themselves into orbit, unlimited.

# Chapter 12

## Turning a New Leaf

before I fall in love
with lethargy

## WITH OPEN HANDS

Hair grey
skin withered
dried by many suns
kissed by the shifting winds

I walk with open hands
feel the spring air
for balmy gentleness

Legs wobbly from following
too many directions
toddle towards beauty of a carmine poppy

a child learning to walk
through swaying stalks of wheat
meadow undulating under its feet

Clouded eyes
skim the clouds to unclad the sunshine
feel it blaze within and without

ears, ever more insular
listen to the coloratura of birds
a chirping flow of joy

in this evening of life
on this gingerly walk
through a familiar carpet
of hopeful streets

## I AM OLD BUT DO NOT FEEL SO

Ha, declares the mirror, life has its limits
you are old.

I ignore it. I am inside my dream-garden
full of pale-green fragile primroses.
It is spring again. The morning breeze
caresses the grass and the grass caresses
my bare feet.

Down the path among the weeds
I walk deeper in time—wild roses
exude scented offerings
to the temple of summer.
The sun leaning down on fields
urges nature to mature
furrows earth's crust
and speaks to ears of corn.

Deeper, deeper—
the aroma of ripening fruit mixes with
late summer flowers. In my garden
plants do not age-discriminate.
Some barely shooting, some fully open
some with limbs become transparent
veiny, needy of consideration
as they verge on their winter.

And still I don't see it coming.
I say I do, but I do not—the inevitable
cold end of the cycle is for somebody else.

I wander off looking for violets.
Not so conscious of the seasons
they bloom twice, thrice, or continuously.

My little models, my darlings. I tell them
all about my dreams and failures and
how I'd love to borrow their breath.

I pluck a few bunches, roots, soil and all
plant them in a vase of amber, make them
face the mirror, survive winter. They tell me
they want to be remembered, and so do I.

By the family I raised.
By the aroma of cakes I baked. By the words
I said or wrote, or by the mute ones, those that
I acted on most often—the incongruent
unreasonable ones—always more memorable.

Remembered by anyone—a passerby
who noticed my scarf grazed ground
and told me so without knowing my name.
Nor do I know his, but I still remember him.

By a child whose roll-away ball I fetched
and handed it back.

By roads travelled or not, mapped, planned
or accidental. I believe that roads have memory.
It all makes beautiful sense now. My life is
a thousand lives and many more opportunities.

Ha, I say, mirror, life has no limits
you have it wrong!

## TURNING A NEW LEAF
*With a nod to Ivan Goncharov*

I need a clean page to start with—
Not a single incidental line
Nor a smudge should distract me—
I, the Oblomov woman of the liquid hours

Vapid days, languishing in sleepy indoors
Lounging on a duvet of excuses
Swaying in the shallow mores
Of undecided pathways.

> Outside, a brilliant day illuminates
> The most secluded crannies, poking
> Mercilessly, waking up promises.

I squeeze my eyelids to keep out the sun
I lower the shades to keep out the life
But I am too late—my porous cocoon
Pierced by persevering light.

> Through the window, a garden green
> Fresh, expectant, keen. The flowers to be
> Cared for, an empty terrace to adorn.

I ask myself what's anchored me so
I tell myself not to wait another minute
To make a small angle of joy possible
On this side of heaven.

Oh truthful age, oh scale of experience
Condemn me for what I have not done.
Reach into the well of my will—there is still
Time before I fall in love with lethargy.

On the terrace, a watering can.
On the table, a ready pen
And an open spiral notebook.

Slower, yes, forgetful, yes. What of it?

A turtle can always win
A race with itself and so shall I.
A crowded page is fine.

I'll write on the edge, turn the page.
And if I deplete the paper
I'll continue writing in my head.
And if I run out of ideas

>   I will visit the garden and observe
>   The tiny critters running tirelessly
>   Their heedless errands, busy
>   On the shiny highway of the leaves.

## A BEAUTIFUL CONFLUENCE

The weight of future generations
pressing on my matrix-shoulders
I felt an urge to invent a wheel
to grapple with the enigma of life—
no solutions but a hedgerow of events
encumbered by the original sin
of inadequate intelligence.

I wished I were born in a previous century
or in the future, in some other place!
I know now, it would not have mattered—
we pass through the press of the same flour mill—
smiles temper rough edges
abuses break the teeth of an advancing cogwheel.

As I floundered through the puzzle of living
with unbending zeal of a young poplar
my eager youth escaped on eager wings
leaving behind an ache for open spaces
undulating meadows, chamomile patches.

Gradually, the skin on the face relaxes—
battles of life simmer on the back burner
from which peace begins to gleam
awareness grows, ebbs, turns to dreams.

My hazel eyes gaze into yours—
we are fading into the same landscape.
Our aging hair blooms with silver filigree
limbs turn heavy like caryatids
as dependence, even innocence returns
to our more childlike faces.

May we then hear our children say
*Mom and Dad would now do this, say that*
and without making much difference
call us, in a word, **Momandad**.

**PASSAGE**

A few more years
to shuffle along old paths
listen to friends reminisce
carve the highlights of life
into a memoir

Hurry!
Fold another paper airplane
hand it to a beloved child
deliver advice—
a desperate bid to give
and leave more behind
to ease the leaving

*Oma, you have such soft skin
but it's so different from mine*

*Yes, my darling, yours
has the softness of apple blossom
—mine of an apple left
on the tree too long*

The child runs away
with questions and giggles
and I am left alone with my age

Fear flaps against my rib cage
Someday the unknown will come
—a violent fall without a safety net
a crash, a last spasmodic pain
or a sheet of silent snowflakes
falling from windless sky
obliterating the landscape

## SEED PODS UNDER MY FEET

What to expect from myself lately
except to begin to forget. It's natural.

The thoughts of this sort pursue me
as vines pursue a crumbling wall.

I feared age would make it hard
to reflect. It does not. Reflecting

like the fumes of fine wine
rises above details, labels;

it mulls over rooted feelings
flies on daring wings, but to find

the precious, precise threads
to weave into a spread of poems

can be daunting. I tell myself
look inward, indulge in the fruit

intact in your heart. Open wide
your wrinkled hands—words

buried deep between the slits
of arthritic joints, live there

precariously like wild columbine
ardently embracing steep cliffs—

do not let them slip—support them
with synonyms and similes

plant the new seeds in gently
cultivated groves of thoughts

clothe a message with a freshly
minted metaphor, and take off.

When the search is earnest
the find will be honest—

a generous display
of exuberance and sorrow.

Last night's shoot will
grow today's sapling and

the playful piping of a robin
will rise out of yesterday's silence.

This harvest I shall humbly deliver
grateful for the language of alternatives.

The seed pods, impatient
bursting under my feet.

# Notes

**Wild Strawberries in Winter** [Page 6] – The title refers to a Slavic tale *Twelve Months* in which a wicked woman banishes her stepdaughter to look for wild strawberries in the middle of the winter, an impossible errand that turns out to be her fortune. It was my favorite fairy tale.

*Euterpe* is one of the Nine Muses in Greek mythology: a goddess of lyric poetry depicted playing a double flute and often referred to as a Giver of Delight.

**Olive Tree (*Maslina*)** [Page 41] – An excerpt from a beloved poem by a revered Croatian poet, writer, and translator Vladimir Nazor (1876-1949). The poem celebrates the spirit and beauty of the Istrian countryside and its influence on the poet.

**Istria of Yore** [Page 42] – A peninsula of Croatia in the North Adriatic Sea where my paternal family came from. My grandfather owned a vineyard and an olive grove there.

**A Blue Fan** [Page 46] – *Rovinj* is a name of an ancient coastal city in Istria, a destination for my summer vacations as a teenager.

**Orlando** [Page 58] – A novel by Virginia Woolf that inspired this poem and was made into a film of the same name.

**A Glimmer of Hope** [Page 96] – The poem mentions Sergei Eisenstein, the Russian film director famed for his masterpiece *Battleship Potemkin* which depicts a mutiny that was considered a precursor of the Russian Revolution. The film contains one of the most powerful scenes in the history of cinematography, a baby carriage rolling down the Odessa Steps.

**At the Edge of Irony** [Page 106] – The poem alludes to the *Sybils*, the priestesses in Greek mythology who often delivered ambiguously crafted prophecies. The fifth stanza in the poem echoes the play of words delivered by the famous *Oracle* *of Dodona* regarding the outcome of a specific battle that is contained in the phrase:

*Ibis redibis nunquam per bella peribis*

The phrase is translated as:

*You will go, you will return, you will never perish in the war.*

or

*You will go, you will return never, you will perish in the war.*

**Turning a New Leaf** [Page 138] – The poem refers to *Oblomov*, a central character in the novel *Oblomov* by the Russian author Ivan Goncharov. The name epitomizes a person whose laziness and indecision ruin his life.

# Acknowledgements

First and foremost, I thank my family—the dear departed ones who inhabit my poems, my husband and our children who are my nourishment here in the present, and our grandchildren who are my hope for the future.

++++

I am grateful to Robert Perry of Dutch Poet Press and Robert Perry Book Design. With his creative skills and understanding, he has been instrumental in bringing this book into being through his editing and design, as well as managing production and distribution.

To poet Phyllis Klein, I thank her for the boundless generosity, insight and expertise she brought to the project of editing the book's manuscript.

To poet and teacher Charlotte Muse, I offer my deep appreciation for her instruction and advice on the art of poetry through her workshop and kind attention and support.

I convey my very special thanks to poet Jane Kos whose friendship and encouragement have fostered my growth as a poet. For this and more, the poems in this volume about Istria are dedicated to her.

I offer my heartfelt appreciation to the people and groups who share my love and devotion to poetry and have provided me with wonderful inspiration and support over the years.

To my friends at the Cupertino poetry circle with leader Ron Miller—before I met you I read my poetry to myself alone.

To my friends at Waverley Writers of Palo Alto; The Not Yet Dead Poets Society at the Main Gallery in Redwood City; Coastside Poetry in Half Moon Bay; and Belmont Poetry Nights. You have been a beacon of poetry and friendship during the last two difficult years with regular opportunities to read and listen.

I'm grateful to all who listened to my readings, because you are the audience I cherish, the hearts I hope to touch.

My special thanks to those who made them happen: Mary-Marcia Casoly, Charlotte Muse and Patrick Daly, Diane Lee Moomey and Steve Long, Ron Miller, Jackie Rigoni and Monica Korde.

# COLOPHON

Cover and interior pages designed by Robert Perry Robert Perry Book Design and Dutch Poet Press.

Printed and distributed by IngramSpark.

Display and Body text set in Palatino designed by Herman Zapf who was attuned to the natural world as the poet of this volume of poetry is.

The photographs on the cover and title page were taken by the author.

www.ingramcontent.com/pod-product-compliance
Lightning Source LLC
Chambersburg PA
CBHW060358080526
44583CB00012B/368